John Bosco

||||||||||||||||||||||||||||||||||||||||||||||||||||

Champion for Youth

Happy 8th Birthday, Ella! Love, Grandma + Grandpa Frey

1815–1888
Born in Becchi, Italy (near Turin)
Feast Day: January 31
Family Connection:
Boys and Schoolchildren

Text by Barbara Yoffie
Illustrated by Katherine A. Borgatti

Liguori

ONE LIGUORI DRIVE
LIGUORI MO 63057-9999

Dedication

To my family:
my parents Jim and Peg,
my husband Bill,
our son Sam and daughter-in-law Erin,
and our precious grandchildren
Ben, Lucas, and Andrew

To all the children I have had the privilege of
teaching throughout the years.

Imprimi Potest:
Harry Grile, CSsR, Provincial
Denver Province, The Redemptorists

Published by Liguori Publications
Liguori, Missouri 63057

To order, visit Liguori.org or call 800-325-9521.

p ISBN 978-0-7648-2290-2
e ISBN 978-0-7648-6909-9

Liguori Publications, a nonprofit corporation, is an apostolate of The
Redemptorists. To learn more about The Redemptorists, visit Redemptorists.com.

Printed in the United States of America
18 17 16 15 14 / 5 4 3 2 1
First Edition

Dear Parents and Teachers:

Saints and Me! is a series of children's books about saints, with six books in each set. The first set, *Saints of North America,* honors holy men and women who blessed and served the land we call home. The second set, *Saints of Christmas,* includes heavenly heroes who inspire us through Advent and Christmas and teach us to love the Infant Jesus.

Saints for Families introduces the virtuous lives of seven saints from different times and places who modeled God's love and charity within and for families. Saint Thérèse of Lisieux felt the love of her family and carried it into her religious community (which included her sisters). Saint Anthony of Padua is the patron of infants and children. Saint John Bosco cared for young, homeless boys, raising them like sons. Saint Thomas More, a father of five, imitated Christ's sacrificial love and devotion to the truth until death. Saints Joachim and Anne became the grandparents of Jesus, raising Mary as a sinless disciple. And Saint Gerard Majella, the patron of pregnant mothers, blessed families with food, knowledge, penances, and healing miracles.

Which saint stood up against a king? Who became a tailor and priest? Which saint is "the little flower?" Who was known for his excellent preaching? Which saints lived before Jesus? Which saint climbed trees, did flips, and turned cartwheels? Find out in the *Saints for Families* set—part of the *Saints and Me!* series—and help your child connect to the lives of the saints.

Introduce your children or students to the *Saints and Me!* series as they:

—READ about the lives of the saints and are inspired by their stories.

—PRAY to the saints for their intercession.

—CELEBRATE the saints and relate to their lives.

John Bosco
1815–1888
Born: Becchi, Italy

Joachim and Anne
First century BC
Born: Nazareth (Joachim) Bethlehem (Anne)

Anthony of Padua
1195–1231
Born: Lisbon, Portugal

Gerard Majella
1726–1755
Born: Muro, Italy

Thérèse of Lisieux
1873–1897
Born: Alençon, France

Thomas More
1478–1535
Born: London, England

The Bosco family lived on a small farm near the city of Turin, Italy. Francis and Margaret Bosco had three sons: Anthony, Joseph, and John. Life on the farm was not easy. There were many jobs to do.

John was only two years old when his father died. His mother worked hard to keep her little family happy and safe. They did not have a lot of money, but they had each other.

They also had faith in God. Margaret told her children stories about God. "God wants us to help other people," she said. John listened to his mother. He liked to pray and go to church.

When John was nine years old, he had a dream. He saw many boys shouting and pushing each other. John tried to stop the rough play. A voice told him to be kind and gentle. He never forgot his dream. What did it mean?

One warm day, John was playing with his friends near a big tree. "Look at me!" he shouted. He climbed on a low branch and hung upside down. Then he jumped to the ground and did a handstand! Everyone clapped.

John told his friends, "I will do more tricks for you. But we should pray first." The boys prayed together. John jumped up and did a cartwheel and a flip in the air! *We can play* and *pray,* he thought.

For a long time, John knew he wanted to be a priest. As a young man, he joined the seminary and was ordained. His mother was very happy and proud of her son. "Be a good and faithful priest," she told him.

As a priest, John was known as Don Bosco. In Italy, "Don" is a special name that means "Father." Don Bosco walked the streets of Turin. He saw many homeless boys. They were hungry and afraid. They did not go to school. Don Bosco knew he could help them.

One Sunday, he asked some boys to come to Mass. After Mass, they ate breakfast and went for a walk. They played tag in a small grassy field. Don Bosco told them stories about God. "I can teach you how to pray," he said.

The boys liked Don Bosco. He was patient and kind. He made them feel special. "Let's tell our friends about this nice priest," said one of the boys. More boys joined the group the next Sunday.

After a short time, the group got very large. Don Bosco had to find more space. He bought a shed and later a small house. The boys had a safe place to stay. Don Bosco's mother became the housekeeper. She cooked and sewed for the boys.

"Dear God, help me to take care of these boys," prayed Don Bosco. He had so much to do! First, he opened a small school. Later, he started classes that taught them how to do different jobs. They learned how to be carpenters, shoemakers, tailors, and printers.

Don Bosco taught the boys about the Catholic faith. They went to Mass every day, and he heard their confessions. He told them, "Do kind deeds for Jesus."

All of Don Bosco's work was done with kindness and love. He wrote books to teach people how to be good Catholics. He taught teachers to respect and love their students.

Don Bosco started a religious order of priests and brothers called the Salesians. There is also a group of Salesian sisters. Today they continue the good work of Don Bosco in countries all over the world.

On January 31, 1888, Don Bosco died at age seventy-two. He told his friends, "Tell the boys I will see them in heaven." Canonized in 1934 by Pope Pius XI, Saint John Bosco is the patron saint of young people, editors, and Catholic publishers.

Let us be patient; let us be kind.
Touch a child's heart, his soul, and his mind.

Dear God.

I love you very much.

Saint John Bosco

loved you, too.

He saw the good

in everyone.

Teach me to be

kind and patient.

Help me to care

for others.

Amen.

NEW WORDS (Glossary)

Canonize: To officially declare that a person is a saint in heaven

Champion: Someone who defends or stands up for another person

Don: "Father" in Italian

Ordained: To receive the sacrament of holy orders and become a priest

Salesians: A religious order that was founded by Saint John Bosco in 1859

Salesian sisters: A group of women religious that was founded by Saint John Bosco and Saint Mary Mazzarello in 1872

Seminary: A school where men are trained to become priests

Saint John Bosco also has been honored as a saint for magicians. In 2002, Pope Saint John Paul II was asked to declare him the official patron saint of stage magicians.

Liguori Publications
saints and me! series
SAINTS FOR FAMILIES

Collect the entire set!

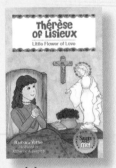

ANTHONY OF PADUA

wonder worker

JOHN BOSCO

champion for youth

THÉRÈSE OF LISIEUX

Little Flower of Love

Joachim and Anne

Love for generations

gerard majella

guardian of mothers

Thomas more

faith-filled father

**SAINTS FOR FAMILIES
ACTIVITY BOOK**

Reproducible activites for all
6 books in the series